PEOPLE IN COSTUME

The Tudors

JENNIFER RUBY

B.T. Batsford Ltd · London

First published 1995

Typeset by Goodfellow & Egan Ltd, Cambridge
and printed in Hong Kong by Colorcraft Ltd

Published by
B.T. Batsford Ltd
4 Fitzhardinge Street
London W1H 0AH

A CIP catalogue record for this book is available from the
British Library

ISBN 0 7134 7214 6

CONTENTS

1520

INTRODUCTION

In Tudor times, life was very different from today. There were no big housing estates, factories, cars, aeroplanes or machines. Instead there were vast areas of open countryside with small towns and tiny villages. People did not travel very far and as there were no telephones, televisions or fast postal services, communication was very slow.

The royal family and the nobles were the most important people in the land and they set the fashion in clothes. These fashions were copied by those rich enough to afford them. However, many people living deep in the countryside would have no idea of what was fashionable at court. Poor people had to struggle to buy food and to keep a roof over their heads so they would not be interested in fashion.

In this book you will meet many different characters and you can compare their clothes and lifestyles. Let us begin by talking to a Joker.

'Hello, I am the Joker from a pack of playing cards. I am wearing a parti-coloured* suit and hat decorated with bells and my shoes have long points. Most court jesters or jokers wear an outfit like mine. The Tudors love to play cards. If you get out a pack of playing cards today, you will find that the Queens are still pictured wearing a gable headdress, which is a Tudor fashion. Now I am going to take you on a journey back in time to the sixteenth century so that you can learn all about the clothes worn by people in Tudor England.'

*parti-coloured is when a garment is made half in one colour and half in another.

1500: A CASTLE

Let us imagine that the year is 1500 and we are visiting a castle deep in the countryside.

This is Martha, a serving maid, who lives and works in the castle. She is wearing a hood with slits up the sides which covers most of her hair. Her gown is very plain and is made of a coarse linen material. She has knotted the skirt up out of the way while she is working and you can see that she has another gown on underneath.

On the opposite page there is a picture of Albert the cook and his wife.

Albert is wearing a tunic and leggings and he has a cloth tucked into his waist as an apron. His wife is wearing a gown with two brooches fastening the neckline in place. Her headdress is more elaborate than Martha's and she has a cloak draped over one shoulder. Can you find out what kind of meals they might cook?

Martha

Albert

LADIES' FASHIONS

Here are two noblewomen who live in the castle.

Cecily is wearing a blue velvet dress with a square neck and tight sleeves. The sleeves have been cut from the wrist to the elbow so that her white chemise (a kind of smock) shows through. Making cuts in a garment like this is called slashing. Cecily has a jewelled belt at her waist and she has hitched up her skirt at the back. It is fastened at the back of her waist with another jewel.

Cecily

8

Letitia is wearing a brown velvet gown that is lined with fur. There are laces across the back and she has also hitched her skirt up. You can see her patterned undergown which is made of silk. Both ladies are wearing dark hoods which have hanging pieces at the back and sides.

Letitia

A HARP PLAYER

The noblemen and women like to be entertained, especially when they are eating. Joel often plays his harp and sings at the large banquets held at the castle.

He is wearing a tunic with a belt at the waist. The sleeves have dagged edges. This means that the material has been cut into a pattern. He is also wearing a flat cap, tights and soft leather shoes. He has a silver garter around his right knee. In Tudor times, tights were called hose and were made of cloth not elastic.

What other musicians might be at the castle?

Joel

A LADY-IN-WAITING

Mary is lady-in-waiting to Letitia. Letitia often gives her old gowns to Mary so she is usually beautifully dressed although not quite as extravagantly as her mistress.

Here she is wearing a black hood with a decorated front and a plain gown which she is holding up at the front to enable her to walk more freely. You can see that she has another gown on underneath. Why do you think ladies wore so many clothes?

Mary

MEN'S FASHIONS

This is Edmund, Letitia's husband. He is a rich duke and owns the castle and all the surrounding land. He often entertains King Henry VII so he is up-to-date with the fashions worn by those at court.

He is wearing a long gown that is richly embroidered. It has slashed sleeves and underneath you can see his doublet. A doublet is a kind of close-fitting jacket worn by men. Edmund's doublet is very short and also has slashed sleeves. Underneath the doublet, he is wearing a white shirt with a low neck. He also has on a flat cap, hose and velvet shoes.

Edmund

This is Hal, Edmund's younger brother, who is playing a lute. He is wearing a black velvet cap with a turned-up brim of red silk, a white shirt and a black velvet doublet. The sleeves of his doublet have been slashed in several places and tied together with laces. These laces are called points. If you look at the accessories on page 46, you can see these illustrated in more detail.

Hal has a cloak around his shoulders and a black leather purse hanging from his waist. His shoes are made of black velvet and he has a jewelled garter on one knee.

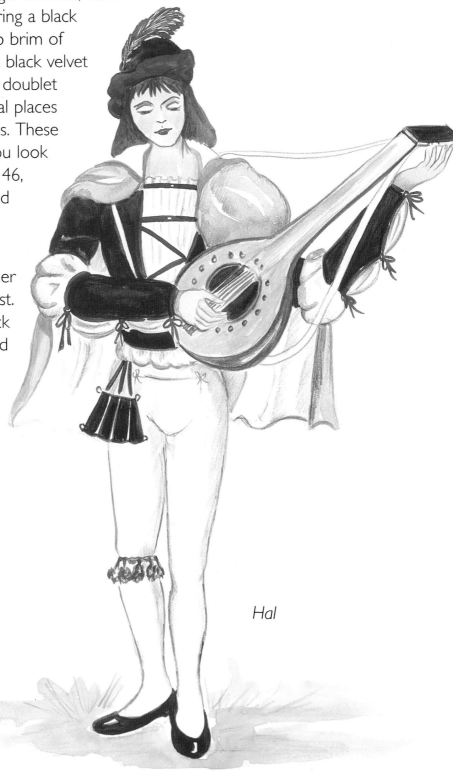

Hal

FARM WORKERS

William is a farmer on the duke's estate. He has little time for fashion and his clothes are plain, sturdy and practical.

He is wearing a soft hat and a canvas jerkin* over a coarse linen shirt. He has overstockings on top of his hose and his thick-soled leather boots are fastened with tabs at the front. He carries a leather bag and a knife.

William

*a jerkin is a close-fitting jacket without a collar or sleeves

His wife Alice is working in the fields. She is wearing a straw hat over a wimple. A wimple is a veil worn over the neck and chin and is a fashion from Medieval times. She has hitched up her overskirt so that it is out of the way while she is working. You can see that she has two underskirts on underneath. Her shoes are made of rushes.

Alice

1530: HAMPTON COURT PALACE

Now we will move forward to the year 1530 and visit Hampton Court Palace to look at what people are wearing. These two ladies are walking in the herb garden of the palace. They are both dressed in the latest fashion.

Marguerite is wearing a red gown with wide sleeves. It has a low square neck and an opening at the front through which you can see her gold coloured undergown. The sleeves of her undergown have been slashed, revealing her chemise which she wears next to her skin. She has a pomander containing perfumed spices hanging from the girdle at her waist.

Marguerite

Katherine is wearing a blue velvet gown with fur sleeves. She has a red sash around her waist. Both these ladies are wearing gable hoods. The hood has been given this name because it is shaped like a gable.

It was forbidden by law for anyone but the nobility to wear deep crimson or blue velvet materials at this time.

How do you think people would react today if they were restricted in the colours they were allowed to wear?

Katherine

TWO GARDENERS

The Tudors took great pride in their gardens which were beautifully kept and often arranged in complicated geometric patterns.

Here you can see John, a young boy who is employed to tend the herbs. He is wearing a flat cap, a leather jerkin over a shirt, thick hose and a pair of ankle boots.

His brother Adam is working in another part of the palace grounds. He is wearing a flat cap, a shirt and a tunic that has short sleeves and is belted at the waist. He also has on thick hose and overstockings. His shoes are made of leather.

John

Adam

A RICH MAN AND HIS PAGE

Edward

On the left is Marguerite's husband Edward. He is a rich nobleman and is wearing the latest fashions. If you compare his outfit with that of Edmund on page 12 you will see how much fashions have changed.

The doublet has become much longer and has a kind of skirt. The top parts of the hose are pouched and padded and padding is also used in the shoulders of the gown. The result of this is to give a 'square' look to the fashions of the day. Edward's shirt has a high neck and is beautifully embroidered. He has an ostrich feather in his cap and his shoes are made of leather.

Edward's page is wearing a high-necked shirt, a doublet with a short skirt and hose. He is carrying a pair of Edward's shoes on a velvet cushion. The shoes are made of velvet and have been slashed to reveal their white satin lining.

SWEETENING THE AIR

Gold scent bottle, set with precious stones

Hygiene was poor in Tudor times and there were many unpleasant smells in the home and street. Flowers, herbs and spices were used to disguise these bad odours. Henry VIII often used to walk along with an orange stuffed with cloves held close to his nose and Tudor ladies liked to carry a pomander or scent bottle with them at all times.

On the left you can see Katherine's jewelled scent bottle and below a picture of a herbal fumigator which is used in the palace.

Katherine and her other sister Eleanor are walking in a beautiful rose garden in the palace grounds. Eleanor has her bulky skirt hitched up and secured with two gold clasps at her waist. Only one of these is visible. You can see her squared-toed velvet shoes which are very fashionable. Can you find her tiny perfume bottle suspended from the silk sash around her waist?

As Katherine has her back to you, you can see how the gable hood looks from behind.

A rose was the symbol of the royal family of Tudor. Can you find out how it originated?

The Tudor rose

A herbal fumigator – herbs were burned in here to disguise unpleasant smells

Katherine

Eleanor

1553: The Court of Mary Tudor

We will now move on to the year 1553 and to the court of Mary Tudor. This is Elizabeth, the daughter of a nobleman. In both pictures she is wearing a French hood rather than the gable hood that you saw earlier. Sometimes she wears it decorated with jewels.

Both dresses are tight-waisted and have high necklines. Underneath the dress on the right she is wearing a chemise and a Spanish farthingale. This is an underpetticoat that has hoops put into it to make the dress stand out.

The borders around the armholes on the green dress are for decoration. They are called pickadils.

A Spanish farthingale

It was usual for ladies to carry small posies of flowers at this time. Sometimes Elizabeth likes to wear a posy at her neck as in the picture on the opposite page.

Elizabeth

A RICh MERChANT AND hIS WIFE

Thomas is a rich merchant. He sometimes visits the court of Mary Tudor to sell the beautiful materials that he imports from abroad.

He is wearing a cloak with sleeves and a stand-up collar and a short doublet. Look how padded the top part of the hose has now become! Thomas's hose have panes. These are strips of material that are sewn together at the top and bottom and used for decoration. You can see another illustration of paned hose on page 29.

The fashion for extremely padded hose could be quite inconvenient. It was often difficult for men to sit comfortably in an ordinary chair. Soldiers sometimes used them for storing their loot!

Thomas

Thomas's wife Dorothy is always dressed fashionably. Here she is wearing a French hood and a dress with a standing collar and hanging sleeves. She has a prayer book suspended from her waist on a gold chain. The neck of her chemise is high. This is significant as this fashion will develop into the ruff that will be so popular in Elizabethan times.

In the picture, Dorothy's brooch has been left blank. Can you design a brooch for her? What kind of jewels would it have?

Dorothy

A LORD AND HIS SERVANT

This is Elizabeth's father, Lord Richard.
He is an adviser to the Queen and a
powerful member of her council.

Lord Richard

Lord Richard is wearing a purple jerkin and matching cap and a doublet with sleeves that have been slashed from the shoulder to the wrist. His hose have been paned and padded and he has thigh-length leather boots fastened with straps to his hose. Below, there is a picture of a pair of his hose where you can see the panes more clearly. Special seating had to be put up in the Houses of Parliament because so many men were wearing padded hose and could not sit in the ordinary chairs!

Robin is one of Richard's servants. He is wearing a buff coloured jerkin over a green doublet and hose. His doublet and matching cap are decorated with tiny slashes.

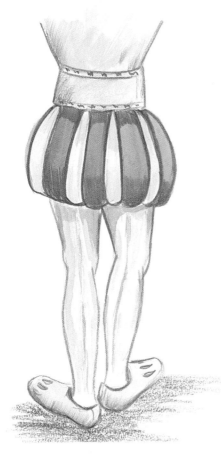

1588: PLYMOUTH

Now it is 1588, the year of the Spanish Armada, and we are in Plymouth. Let us visit one of the busy streets in the town.

Joanna sells apples and eggs on a stall in a street market. She is carrying a basket of her produce to the stall. She is wearing a very plain brown woollen gown and a white apron and has a white linen hood on her head.

On the opposite page you can see Jane, a country woman who has come to buy her groceries. She is wearing a plain gown, a white apron and a small cloak. She has a linen cloth on her head under her hat and a muffler over her mouth. Why do you think she might need this?

Gilbert is reading a letter from Sir Francis Drake who will soon be in Plymouth. Gilbert is wearing a doublet with a 'peascod belly'. This means that it is padded in the front. Gilbert and Jane are both wearing ruffs around their necks.

On the next two pages you can see Gilbert outside the house where he lives and also two of his neighbours. Can you describe their costumes?

Jane

Gilbert

FASHIONS

TOWNSFOLK

In another street in Plymouth we meet Harry, a friend of Gibert's, and also a doctor and his wife.

Harry is wearing a doublet with a peascod belly. It has a buttoned slit in one sleeve which he uses as a pocket. The top part of his hose are quite long and baggy and are called Venetians.

The doctor is wearing a long gown edged with fur, a flat cap and a coif. This is a close fitting linen cap, tied under his chin. He is carrying a bag of potions and has a scroll of prescriptions at his waist.

His wife's gown is open at the front and is tied at the waist with a sash. She is holding a poking stick which is used for resetting ruffs after they have been washed and starched.

On the next two pages you can see the busy harbour and a picture of Sir Francis Drake who successfully defeated the Spanish Armada in 1588. Can you find out more about it?

Harry

SOLDIERS AND SAILORS

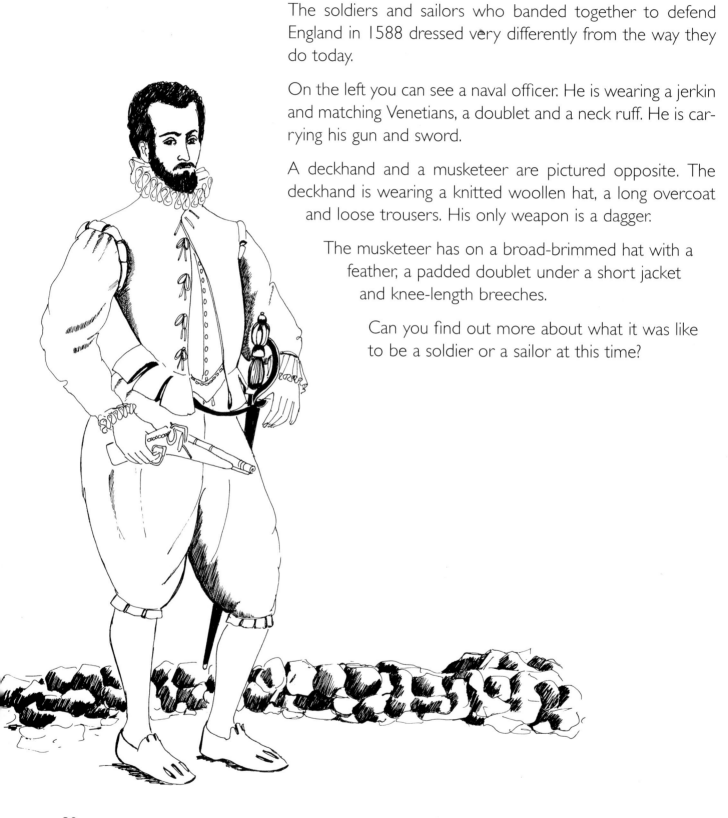

The soldiers and sailors who banded together to defend England in 1588 dressed very differently from the way they do today.

On the left you can see a naval officer. He is wearing a jerkin and matching Venetians, a doublet and a neck ruff. He is carrying his gun and sword.

A deckhand and a musketeer are pictured opposite. The deckhand is wearing a knitted woollen hat, a long overcoat and loose trousers. His only weapon is a dagger.

The musketeer has on a broad-brimmed hat with a feather, a padded doublet under a short jacket and knee-length breeches.

Can you find out more about what it was like to be a soldier or a sailor at this time?

1590: A STRANGE NEW FASHION

The back view

We will now move forward to the end of Queen Elizabeth's reign and look at a rather unusual fashion. This is Lady Anne, a nobleman's wife. You can see that her dress stands out at the hips. This is because she is wearing a petticoat called a French farthingale. The petticoat has a wheel shape inside made of whalebone. This fashionable shape looks very strange from behind. You can compare the shape of the French farthingale with the Spanish farthingale on page 24.

Lady Anne's ruff is very large and is supported by wire at the back. The material of her dress has been richly embroidered. Can you design a beautiful fabric that would be suitable for an Elizabethan lady?

Anne has her hair brushed high off her forehead and has used a pad underneath to give it more volume. She also uses hair dye. It is rumoured that the old Queen wears a wig as her own hair is now white and sparse. Can you find a picture of Queen Elizabeth late in her reign? What do *you* think?

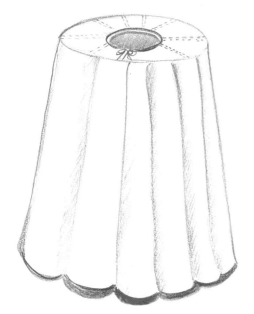

The French farthingale

hEADDRESSES AND hAIRSTYLES

On these two pages you can see examples of headdresses and hairstyles from Tudor times. Which is the style that is still worn by the Queens in a pack of playing cards today?

1520

1530

1585

1586

1563

1575

1517

CHILDREN'S CLOTHES

1539

In Tudor times, children were dressed like adults. Can you imagine how hot and uncomfortable this must have been?

On the far left is a picture of Prince Edward when he was two years old. His gown and matching hat do not look very suitable for playing in.

1590

Girl, age 5

Both the little girls pictured here are wearing very tight-fitting dresses and decorated caps. Why might it be unhealthy for children to wear clothes like this?

1577

Girl, age 3

ACCESSORIES

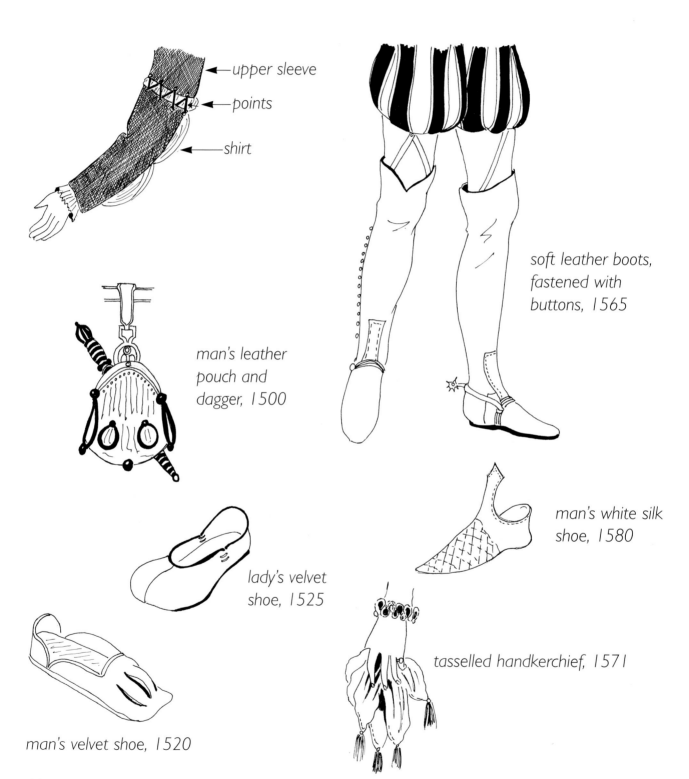

upper sleeve

points

shirt

soft leather boots,
fastened with
buttons, 1565

man's leather
pouch and
dagger, 1500

man's white silk
shoe, 1580

lady's velvet
shoe, 1525

tasselled handkerchief, 1571

man's velvet shoe, 1520

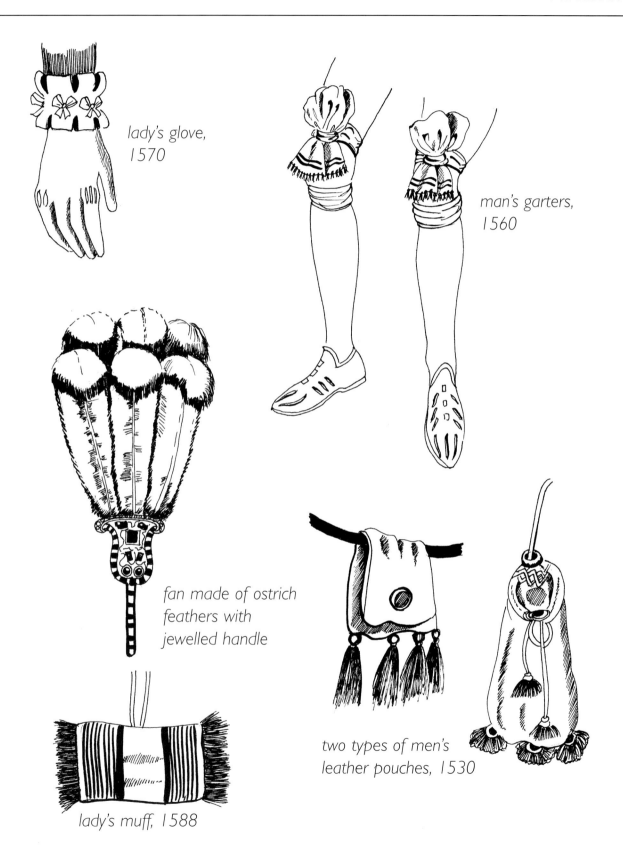

lady's glove,
1570

man's garters,
1560

fan made of ostrich
feathers with
jewelled handle

two types of men's
leather pouches, 1530

lady's muff, 1588

INDEX AND GLOSSARY